SAVINGS ON MOTOR INSURANCE

Mohammed Sadullah Khan

Copyright © 2012 Mohammed Sadullah Khan
All rights reserved.
ISBN-13: 978-1502476845
ISBN-10: 1502476843

DEDICATION

This book is dedicated to the memory of my mother, Asifa Begum.

Quick ways of Understanding Motor Insurance

Due to globalization and rapid increase in the purchasing power of the people we find that the number of vehicle's on road have increased tremendously. There were no cars in my colony back in India some 30 years ago. Now a day's house owners are struggling to find a parking space in the same colony.

The Insurance Companies have also mushroomed. It is difficult to find a right Insurer offering the right product and service. There are also product variations and service variations depending upon the type of country you are living in.

Strong efforts have taken to see to it that the basics of Motor Insurance are covered. Principles of Insurance are also explained in-order to have a better understanding of the Insurance. The covers have been explained at different levels.

The final and crux of the material which is "Savings on Motor Insurance" is dealt with from a variety of angles.

Apart from gaining the knowledge about the basics of Insurance, one should also do adequate research about the breed and culture of the Insurance Company, in-order to get the best out of them.

Mohammed Sadullah Khan

Riyadh, Saudi Arabia,

SAVINGS ON MOTOR INSURANCE

Table of Contents

S.No.	INDEX	PAGE No.
1.	INTRODUCTION	9-13
2.	PRINCIPLES OF INSURANCE	14-23

    a) Utmost Good Faith
    b) Insurance Interest
    c) Indemnity
    d) Subrogation
    e) Contribution
    f) Proximate Cause

3.	MOTOR INSURANCE COVERS	24-28

    a) Third Party Insurance
    b) Third Party Fire and

       Theft coverage
- c) Comprehensive Specified Risk
- d) Comprehensive All Risks Cover

4.   OPTIONAL COVERS   29-33

- a) Dealer Repair Option
- b) Personal Accident Coverage
- c) Medical Expenses Coverage
- d) Geographical Clause
- e) Rent a Car Option

5.   SAVINGS POTENTIAL   34-44

- a) Insured Estimated Value
- b) Deductible or Excess
- c) Un-used Vehicles
- d) Geographical Extension
- e) Personal Accident Coverage
- f) Old Vehicle Insurance

     g) Deletion of Vehicles
     h) Profit-Sharing Clause

6.   CONCLUSION   45-46

***

1. INTRODUCTION

Motor Insurance is also know by its other names like Automobile or Auto Insurance, Vehicle Insurance and sometimes by the name of the vehicle like Car Insurance, Bike Insurance, Two wheeler Insurance, Commercial Vehicle Insurance, Private Car Insurance.

The vehicles on the roads are increasing with the passing of each day. The weather pattern is also changing the world-over and causing losses in different forms. The congestion on the roads is leading to numerous small accidents.

Motor is considered as a dangerous animal as it causes death, injuries and property damages and it is supposed to be insured against loss it causes. Almost all the countries in the world have a mandatory Motor Insurance.

The purpose of the Mandatory Insurance is to cover the third party liabilities arising out of use of Motor Vehicle. The Mandatory Insurance makes it compulsory for each and every entity owning a Motor vehicle to have a minimum Third Party insurance.

During my 25 years of experience I found that due to lack of understanding of Motor Insurance many Individuals and Corporations were losing a lot of money.

Motor Insurance in some countries is the largest Insurance Portfolio. But in a vast number of countries it ranks in the top 3 in terms of volume, which is understood as GWP (Gross working Premiums). Even if we take the case of vast majority of individuals or corporate, Motor Insurance forms the bulk of their Insurance portfolio.

For some Insurance Companies Motor Insurance is not an attractive class of business as it causes loss. It is also known as attrition class of business.

From the financial angle if we look there are individuals who pay a premium of as low a US $ 25 and there are corporations who end up paying a premium of over US $ 100 million a year. In order get the most out of Motor Insurance, one should have a full and right understanding of it.

A proper reading of this book will help in understanding the intricacies of Motor Insurance. Focusing the needs and requirements of laymen it provides information useful even to the experts in Motor Insurance.

The book will be useful to buyers of the Motor/Car/Vehicle insurance. It is also useful to the Insurance Companies, the providers of Insurance, teachers and students of Insurance.

It provides valuable information on how the savings can be made by taking decisions proactively on Motor Insurance. A scientific and logical guide to Motor Insurance, if properly used can make a substantial savings.

2. PRINCIPLES OF INSURANCE

As the insurance evolved few centuries earlier, with its evolution the principles guiding the Insurance also evolved. Justice cannot be done to any topic on insurance without the understanding of these principles. There are six principles of Insurance, which are as follows,

a) Utmost Good Faith
b) Insurance Interest
c) Indemnity
d) Subrogation
e) Contribution
f) Proximate Cause

a) Utmost Good Faith

We will try to understand each one of the above principles. First and the foremost principle is known as the Principle of Utmost Good Faith.

In product marketing we abide by the principle of Good Faith. Suppose you are buying a Refrigerator you go to the showroom and buy the product by paying the price quoted by the Salesman and you are not disclosing any information related to you or your activities. Even the Salesman is not supposed to disclose any information unless asked for and if any information is asked by the client then he is supposed to provide the right information. It is guided by the principle of "let the buyer beware" or in Latin it is called as "Caveat Emptor".

If you are hiring a taxi, you ask the driver to take him to a particular location and he will quote his price without him interested in knowing anything about you. You are also not interested in asking about him and his antecedents. Once he drops you to the place agreed upon you till pay the amount agreed.

But Insurance contracts are over and above this. They are termed as contracts of Utmost Good Faith. Utmost Good faith is nothing but it is duty of disclosure. What needs to be disclosed is the question, which comes to our mind. We need to disclose all the information which helps the insurers in taking decision whether to insure us or to reject our proposal. If he is accepting the proposal then the information helps him in providing the terms and conditions to the policy. Hence it is very essential that all the information should be provided to the Insurers.

There is a saying that we should provide the right information to Doctors, Lawyers and Insurers. This holds good and true. Not providing the correct information may jeopardize your contract. In-case of doubt as to whether to provide the information to the Insurer, it is better to provide the information.

Duty of Utmost good faith is applicable to all the parties to the Insurance Contract. The Insurance company should also provide the information related to its products its terms and conditions. A customer may be able to take a knowledgeable decision if he has the right information. Hence it is required on part of the insurer to provide the right and detailed information to the insured.

For individual most of the insurance companies insist upon submission of proposal forms which contain sufficient information related to Utmost Good Faith. Some forms also contain information as to what need to be disclosed before and during the currency period of the contract.

b) Insurance Interest

The second most important principle of Insurance is Insurance Interest. A person without insurable interest cannot buy insurance policy.

If we want to understand from a laymen's perspective Insurable Interest is simply Ownership. You have insurable interest if you own the item or subject matter to be insured. But on a broader front without ownership if you have financial interest then it is considered as an insurable interest. The entity who is staking a claim under the policy should be the person suffering the financial loss. This gives wider scope to the understanding of the principle of Insurable Interest. The Garages, which are handling the vehicles belonging to the customers, can cover the vehicles of the customer in-spite of them being not the owners of the vehicle.

c) Indemnity

It is the third most important principle of Insurance and comes into play when there is a claim. The principle of Indemnity states that the person suffering the financial loss should be compensated equal to the loss he suffered. He should in the same financial position after the loss as he was before the loss.

Suppose a Car meets with an accident and if one of its door is damaged and the cost of replacement of the door with labor charges is US $ 3,000. Then he should be paid US $ 3,000. But in practice this may not happen as policies have conditions like deductible or excess and depreciation condition. However the spirit of the principle should be followed in the process of Insurance. The insured should not be better off nor worse off from the accident.

On the other hand if there is a deductible of US$ 500 then the claims will be settled for US $ 2500, which will not fully compensate the Insured. Similarly if there is a depreciation clause of say 10% per year and if the accident happens after 2 years of purchase of the vehicle, then the depreciation is deducted from the claim amount apart from excess. The amount net of deductible and excess will be US $ 1,900. Two amounts have been deducted from US $ 3,000, an excess US $ 500 and depreciation US $ 600 (which is 20% of the cost of the door). In practice this principle may not be fully applied in all types of policies.

The following two Principles are supporting the Principle of Indemnity.

➢ Subrogation

➢ Contribution

d) Subrogation

It is one of the sixth principle, which supports the achievement of Indemnity. Suppose any third party is responsible for the damage to Insured car then the Insured has a right to claim from that party that was responsible for the damage to his car, moreover he can also claim from his Insurance Company. This gives the benefit of two claims to the Insured and he will definitely benefit from Insurance. In-order to avoid such a situation, where the Insured is in a better off position thereby violating the principle of Indemnity, Subrogation is applied.

The Insurance Company applies the principle of Subrogation, which will help the Insurance Company recover the damages from the third party on behalf of their Insured. In laymen terms Subrogation is nothing but assuming the legal rights of a person for which the expenses or claim has been paid.

e) Contribution

This is another principle which is supporting the principle of Indemnity. In some cases there are chances that the Insured may buy more than one policy for the same risk.

This may happen due to various reasons, like the CEO may cover the same Vehicle as a part of his personal fleet and the Administration Manager may also cover the same Vehicle as a part of the Company Fleet. Some covers overlap and there may also be a deliberate attempt to commit fraud. Once again if more than one Insurance Company is paying for the same loss then the Insured will be in a beneficial position.

This situation is avoided by applying the principle of Indemnity. The Insurance Companies will not fully compensate the insured against the loss but they share the loss in the proportion of their liability.

This way the insured will not get more than his loss. But by buying more than one policy he loses more premium, thus this principle will discourage the purchase of more than one policy by the insured and restrict the payment of claim so that the insured is not in a better position.

f) Proximate Cause

The last and tricky principle is known as the Proximate Cause. Normally it is difficult to pin point the cause of loss responsible for the loss or damage if there are more than one cause or overlapping causes. The Proximate cause can be the first cause or last cause or may be dominant cause. If earthquake risk is excluded from the policy then if the fire is caused by the earthquake then the risk is excluded even though the damage is caused by the fire risk which is covered in the policy.

There are risks which are insured and some are excluded. To identify whether a claim is payable or not we need to know the cause of loss. Once we know the cause of loss then we will be in a position to say that a particular loss is payable or not. Proximate cause helps us in identifying the root cause of loss in case of more than one cause or overlapping causes of loss.

3. MOTOR INSURANCE COVERS

In Motor Insurance normally the following type of coverage's are available

a) Third Party Insurance
b) Third Party Fire and Theft coverage
c) Comprehensive Specified Risk
d) Comprehensive All Risks Insurance

a) Third Party Insurance

The Third Party Insurance is the basic cover available in the Market for Motor Vehicle, it covers liabilities arising out of usage of the insured motor vehicle. It takes care of liabilities arising out of bodily injury (including death) and liabilities arising out of property damage. It is the cover usually made compulsory by the authorities in almost all the countries of the world. It is also known and Mandatory Motor Insurance cover. Depending upon the countries and companies providing the coverage there may be slight variations but the essence of the coverage is similar.

The intention of this cover is to indemnify the Insured against all sums including claimants costs and expenses, which the Insured shall become legally liable to pay in respect of death or bodily injury to any person and damage to the property occurring during any period of insurance and arising out of an accident caused by, through or in connection with, the Insured vehicle, or the driving by the Insured of a motor vehicle not belonging to or hired (under a hire purchase agreement or otherwise) to him, or his employer, or his partner. The liability limits of death or bodily injury and property damage are separately mentioned in the policy.

b) Third Party Fire and Theft coverage

The next level of coverage is Third Party Fire and Theft coverage. It is usually taken when the vehicle is not in usage and either kept in a Garage or some safe place for a long period. This cover is usually taken if an entity owns more than one vehicle or lack of usage of one or some of the vehicles. The reason may be many like planning to sell one or more vehicles or if there is a plan to go abroad for a long vacation or simply has more than the required number of vehicles and usage is restricted to some vehicles only.

In this apart from the basic Third Party coverage there are additional coverage like loss or damage to the Vehicle by theft or fire and the wording is usually as follows apart from the Third Party wording, "By fire external explosion self-ignition or lightning or burglary housebreaking or theft",.

c) Comprehensive Specified Risks Insurance

The base cover under Comprehensive Insurance is Comprehensive Specified Risks. Under this coverage apart from basic TP Fire and Theft cover, it specifies various other perils which are covered under the policy.

This policy is also known as named perils policy. Only risks which are mentioned are covered under the policy apart from the Third Party coverage.

The wording in the policy is usually as follows,

The Insurance Company will indemnify the Insured against loss of or damage to the Motor Vehicle and its accessories and spare parts whilst thereon

i) by accidental collision or overturning or collision or overturning consequent upon mechanical breakdown or consequent upon wear and tear

ii) by fire external explosion self-ignition or lightning or burglary housebreaking or theft

iii) by malicious act

iv) whilst in transit (including the processes of loading and unloading incidental to such transit) by road rail inland waterway lift or elevator

e) Comprehensive All Risks Cover

The ultimate cover under any motor policy is Comprehensive All Risks Insurance. The policy provides basic third party cover plus damages caused to the insured vehicle by all perils, wherein perils are not specified but exclusions are specified. The usual exclusions are as follows even these are applicable to other Comprehensive covers.

The Company shall not be liable to pay for

i) consequential loss depreciation wear and tear mechanical or electrical breakdowns failures or breakages

ii) damage to tyres unless the Motor Vehicle is damaged at the same time

iii) loss of or damage to accessories or spare parts by burglary housebreaking or theft unless the Motor Vehicle is stolen at the same time.

4. OPTIONAL COVERS

Apart from the core covers there are some additional covers which are offered along with the basic motor insurance.

a) Dealer Repair Option
b) Personal Accident Coverage
c) Medical Expenses Coverage
d) Geographical Clause
e) Rent a Car Option

a) Dealer Repair Option

The foremost is the Dealer repair option cover, this is suitable for vehicles which are brand new and have a warranty from the dealer. This gives an option to the insured to repair his vehicle at the dealer.

But this is costing him additional deductible and may be in certain cases additional premium. Normally a vehicle can be repaired in ordinary work-shop, the cost of repairing at an ordinary garage is cheaper compared to the Dealer Workshop. But if a vehicle is repaired at an ordinary workshop then this may prejudice the warranty of the vehicle which normally is for three years.

b) Personal Accident Coverage

The other extension is for the Personal Accident coverage to the Driver and the Passengers in the car. It is relatively a cheap cover considering the number of accidents and deaths occurring on roads around the World. Normally the coverage is for a sum insured of US $ 100,000 or less. Depending upon the type of country and Company the coverage may be wider or narrower.

A standard Personal Accident Endorsement may provide the following basic coverage.

1. Accidental Death US $ 100,000

2. Total and irrecoverable loss of sight in both eyes US $ 100,000

3. Total and irrecoverable loss of sight in one eye US $ 50,000

4. Loss of limbs US $ 100,000

5. Loss of one limb US $ 50,000

6. Permanent Total Disablement US $ 100,000

Extra Benefits may also be offered like

a) A weekly benefit of US$ 500 per week for Temporary total Disablement may also be provided as additional benefit.

b) Medical expenses cover up-to certain limits.

Most of the companies may provide restricted coverage to spouse and children under PA extension.

c) Medical Expenses Coverage

This is also an optional extension provided by small number of Companies under this Medical expenses are cover. Normal Motor Policies may have automatic Medical expenses cover for Emergency situations covering a very small sum insured. But taking an extension will provide you with a wider coverage may be upto US $100,000.

d) Geographical Clause

Almost all the Motor policies issued have a Geographical/Jurisdiction clause restricting the coverage to the country of Insurance.
Some vehicles which are traveling to foreign countries need to have an extension to get coverage for own damage section of their policy, as most of the countries in the world have mandatory TP (Third Party) cover which need to be purchased from local insurer. Hence TP Insurance can be purchased at borders or from any local Insurer who is authorized to provide the necessary coverage by extending the Geographical Area clause.

e) Rent a Car Option

Now a days due to fast pace of life car has become a necessity. In-order to see to it that the vehicle owner financial loss is restricted the Insurer's offer rent a Car option to the Insured whose vehicle is damaged and in the Garage for repairs. This may also be an extra option or may be a built in cover depending upon the Country and the Company offering the service.

5. SAVINGS POTENTIAL

There are various ways of making a savings on Motor Insurance if we plan properly, scientifically and proactively.

The areas in which the savings can be made are as follows,

a) Insured Estimated Value

b) Deductible or Excess

c) Un-used Vehicles

d) Geographical Extension

e) Personal Accident Coverage

f) Old Vehicle Insurance

g) Deletion of Vehicles

h) Profit-Sharing Clause

a) Insured Estimated Value

The Insured estimated value of the vehicle is the most important element of motor Insurance rating.

In event of total loss Insurers are bound by the "Principle of Indemnity" and they are supposed to pay the actual loss incurred by the client and not beyond that.

The Insurance Company may not be in a position to judge as to estimate the value of the Vehicle. Many people handling Insurances have little time to look into the intricacies of Insurance and they are pressed for time. When the policy becomes due for renewal, at the end of each policy period they just ask the Insurance Companies to renew their policies on expiring terms. As a method of convenience the Insurance Company may renew the policy as expiring without looking into the valuation aspect or estimation aspect of the risk.

It is important that the persons who are dealing with the Insurance Company are fully aware of the policies of the Insurance Companies with whom they are dealing in respect of partial losses and total loss. Each year at-least three months before the expiry date of the policies, the client should make an assessment of all his vehicles to arrive at a right market value of each and every vehicle. In case of total loss the insured will get the reasonable Market value or sum insured whichever is less. Hence Over-insurance is not helpful to the insured. Similarly under insurance, may also cause problems to the insured especially when the decision is made for settlement of total loss.

Some of the Companies have ended up saving between 20-25% on premiums based on re-evaluation of their vehicles.

b) Deductible or Excess

A deductible is also known as excess in some countries. They are used as synonyms. However, an excess and deductible are slightly different if we look minutely. An excess is an amount a policyholder must bear before the liability passes to the insurer. A deductible is an amount deducted from the claim amount. However as a general rule they are one and same.

Deductible is also a major factor in rating. There are two types of deductible one is Mandatory deductible and the other one is Voluntary deductible. The Mandatory deductible is compulsory and it cannot be removed, whereas the Voluntary deductible is at the option of Insured and if he opts for it then he will get a rebate. The normal range is from US $ 100 to US $ 500, whereas in case of foreign country travel and Agency Repair the deductible range is from US $ 100 to US $ 1000.

A company opting for higher deductible pays lower premium. Hence a quick look into the claims record of the company will help in arriving at a right level of deductible to make a savings in the premiums.

c) Un-used Vehicles

Some companies have a large number of vehicles which are neither sold nor used for over 3 months and subsequently they are sold. This usually happens when the Insured decides to write off or replaces the vehicle with another vehicle and till the time it is sold away to the prospective client it is unused for few months. In such cases they should go in for Third Party Fire and Theft coverage in-order to make a savings in the premium. This will give them a savings of almost over 50% on the premiums of unused vehicles.

d) Geographical Extension

Many big corporations have offices across the countries and some Companies having offices in places closer to the neighboring countries. They usually have business and social dealing with the neighboring countries. This will allow some executives and employees to have regular trips to the neighboring countries. The Insured instead of insuring the vehicles belonging to these personnel, will insure all the vehicles belonging in that particular category of employee and premium is paid accordingly.

A proper evaluation as to who will be traveling to the foreign countries or restricting the coverage to the vehicles which will be traveling outside the Kingdom will plug in the seepage of unnecessary premiums.

e) Personal Accident Coverage

On Personal Accident coverage to Driver and Passengers, this is an optional coverage and is restricted to the usage of the vehicle. This cover is highly recommended cover under normal circumstances. However most of the multi-national companies and highly professional companies provide their employees with full Group Personal Accident and Group Life covers, which are applicable 24 hours a day and will also provide coverage in case of any accidental death and or disability due to vehicular accident. In such cases this cover can be avoided, the savings provided by avoiding this coverage comes to between 3-5%.

f) Old Vehicle Insurance

A regular review of entire fleet should be done at the time of renewal and if any vehicles are found to be valued less than US$ 3,000 or some criteria to be fixed, depending upon the viability. These should be listed separately and can be covered for Third Party Insurance only. This will give them a savings of approximate 50% in this segment.

Most of these are old vehicles and may not warrant repairs for small scratches and dents. In case of total loss, salvage is recoverable hence the quantum of exposure is very less and worth retaining.

g) Deletion of Vehicles

Many corporate clients will have problem with this. When the vehicle is sold the process takes a long time and after the completion of process they neglect to inform the Company and realize only when the renewal is due. This is another area of savings, by timely notifying the Insurance companies about the deletion of the vehicles premium on unexpired period can be saved. Even delay of one month will cost the company approximately 8% of the premium on that particular vehicle. The delay should not be more than 3 days after the sale of the vehicle.

h) Profit-Sharing Clause

The least discussed or rather ignored aspect in motor insurance is profit sharing clause. Motor Insurance is one of the attrition classes of business. Hence most of the Insurance Companies are willing to offer Profit-Sharing clause if requested.

If the Insured is having good claims experience and unable to get a rebate in the Insurance Premium, then he can request his Insurers to offer the Profit Sharing clause so that in case of good claims experience he should get the benefit of good claims ratio. Indirectly this will be useful for the Insurance Company, the Insured and the Society at large. However it is the client who has to proactively take up with his Insurer for incorporation of this clause.

Most of the Companies with good claims ratio will benefit from this clause. If the claims ratios are good then the Companies may end up saving anywhere between 10 to 30% on the premiums.

6. CONCLUSION

Motor Insurance is one of the simplest and highly used types of Insurance. Technological advancements have helped Insurers to have their own Motor Risk Management Tools for rating the risks.

On the Insured side, Individuals clients can directly upon but whereas a vast majority of companies still rely on their Accountants, Human Resources Personnel and to some extent specialists, drawn from Insurance Industry for managing their Motor Insurance. Companies, which have a substantial Motor Premium, should have a dedicated Motor Risk Management Specialist. He should be adequately trained and be able build his own risk management tools in-order to decide about which risks are to be controlled, avoided, retained or transferred (Insurance) to bring about an optimal expense to the Company.

Toning up of internal operations will help in third party recoveries and help in reducing the claim ratios, bringing about much needed cash flow and reduction in premiums. These specialists by managing the portfolio professionally will be able to bring in about a huge savings to their Organizations.

ABOUT THE AUTHOR

Mohammed Sadullah Khan, Faculty Member, Chartered Insurance Practitioner, Insurance Studies Unit, The Institute of Banking (Saudi Arabian Monetary Agency), an MBA, is a Fellow of Insurance Institute of India and a Fellow of Chartered Insurance Institute (UK). Has more than 25 years of experience in the Insurance Industry, of which 18 years in Saudi Arabia.

He can be reached at mosakhan40@gmail.com. www.generalawarenessforall.blogspot.com

www.ingramcontent.com/pod-product-compliance
Lightning Source LLC
Chambersburg PA
CBHW072045190526
45165CB00018B/1742